BORED AF

AN INSPIRATIONAL GUIDE TO BEATING BOREDOM AND LIVING AN AWESOME LIFE NOW

Joseph Aaron

CTW Publishing

Granite City, IL

CTW Publishing
3477 Nameoki Rd #215
Granite City, IL 62040
www.CTWUniversity.com

Book Layout ©2013 BookDesignTemplates.com

Ordering Information:
Quantity sales. Special discounts are available on quantity purchases by corporations, associations, and others. For details, contact the "Special Sales Department" at the address above.

Bored AF/Joseph Aaron. -- 1st ed.
ISBN **978-1519200105**

To Melody, Emily, Alex, and Justus Who Dream (And Sacrifice) To Make the World Better. You Inspire Me.

Table of Contents

Preface 1

Everything In This Book in 324 Words 3

Introduction 7

I Was Bored 11

A Boredom Epiphany 13

A 2-Minute 39-Second Snapshot 17

Watch Your Language 19

Plenty To Do 21

We're Sure – We're Not Sure 25

Tylenol For A Tumor 27

I'm Bored ... Again 29

Go Jump Out Of A Plane 33

Bored Blunts 37

The Most Important Quote In This Book 39

Rebel Without A Cause 41

Making A Name For Yourself 43

Isn't This Normal? 45

Incalculable Damages 47

The Alarm Clock 49

Either You Know Or You Don't Know 51

Dreams & Visions 57

DREAM 61

BIGGER 63

The Finding Yourself Fallacy 65

The Finding Yourself Fallacy (Part 2) 69

The Artist 73

You Can Do Anything You Want 75

Questions 77

EVEN BIGGER 79

Opportunity Of A   Lifetime 81

It's Never Over – The Best You Ever 83

You Can't Do Anything 85

Gifts & Callings 87

Not Gifted – I Suck 89

Giftless 91

I'm Boring 93

Exploration 95

Curiosity 97

Still Stuck? 99

Your Best – Your Duty 103

So Easy A 10-Year-Old Can Do It 105

The Youngest Self-Made Billionaire 109

Dating Not Married 111

Collaboration 113

God, Eyes, And Reflections 117

More Friends 119

Bored Sex 121

Create 125

Failing... 127

Everything I Said In 476 Words......................... 131

Conclusion 135

Change The World 137

Preface

I guess I don't fit in.

I'm just the type of person who believes it's possible.

Some people call that stupid ... Some call it faith.

Whatever you call it, I call it a dream. I want to do something meaningful with my life (we only get one you know).

My dream is that my tombstone epithet will say "He Changed The World."

Seriously ...

I don't want it put on my tombstone so I feel better about my life.

I actually want to <u>change.</u> <u>the.</u> <u>world.</u>

These aren't just words to me. I've put a lot of thought, time, effort, and sacrifice into initiating the change that I want to see as one of the founders of a student movement whose mission is to do just that - change the world.

For me, the most likely way to see the world changed is by partnering with an engaged young adult population.

In my role as lead visionary for our student movement, I've had front-row seats watching a decade of students grow up (kinda).

I see the ones who are now regretful about the life they've led thus far. And, I'm watching others do incredible things.

Here's the deal: Success leaves clues ... and so does failure.

After 10 years, I see patterns emerging.

Of all the issues I could write about to inspire culture and change the world, I've chosen this one.

I'm confident this one issue can make a big impact on your life and on our shared goal of doing something meaningful with our lives.

I want to talk to you about boredom ... well kinda (you'll see what I mean soon).

Everything In This Book in 324 Words

Nearly everything society has taught you about boredom is wrong.

Stay busy.

Find something fun to do.

Find someone to do something with.

Work.

Boredom's just a rite of passage... a part of life. Don't worry about it.

It's all bad advice. It's wrong.

The truth is, because we've marginalized boredom and its role in our lives, we're still struggling to understand it as a society.

But boredom isn't about fun or friends or work or staying busy.

And, I don't think boredom's presence in your life is an accident because you're a victim of an environment with less to do.

Boredom is actually a gift, because boredom pushes you to make a decision.

Its work is to force you into an answer.

No matter how many times you ignore it or delay it's questioning with staying busy or fun or friends or even work, its dull prodding is patient enough to ask you its important question again on another day.

You've been listening to the quack recommendations of a world that does not even understand what boredom is.

You've obeyed the advice and have found yourself in the repetitious cycle of existence that is far from anything you would call "awesome".

This is because you've treated boredom like a disease. A problem in and of itself that must be cured.

But boredom is not the problem.

Despite the cultural conversations questioning its power, boredom doesn't make teens beat up and kill people.

It doesn't force people into drug addiction.

It doesn't get girls pregnant who wouldn't otherwise have given that boy the time of day.

It doesn't make us hang out with the wrong crowd.

But, in treating the pain of boredom with culture's ineffective medications of fun and friends, we miss the truth. More importantly we do harm to those who are caught in boredom's vicious cycle.

Why are we bored?

What should we do about it?

Introduction

"U bored?"

Surprise! This book is not really about boredom.

It's about you.

Boredom is expected.

Until now, very few people have taken the time to consider the scope of boredom's true impact.

Boredom plays an important role, not only in your life, but in culture itself.

After some pretty substantial research, I've come to the conclusion that if you are over the age of 14 or 15 years old and you're bored on a regular basis, you are in danger.

If you're bored, beware.

I'm also convinced when we really understand boredom's role in our lives and respond appropriately, boredom leaves our lives forever.

Like a student who effectively graduates high school, you never have to go back.

You learned its lesson. You graduate to different problems and challenges.

I've got good news for you. By reading this book, you're about to go to the next level in your life.

Beating boredom is just the first step to living your dream life now, but an important one. It's a step many never overcome.

But that won't be your story.

To help you get there, I've broken this short book into two main parts.

Part One is about helping you to beat boredom. Part Two helps you live an awesome life starting now.

In Part One, we'll get you past merely talking about boredom to a place where you've thought about boredom's surprising role in culture at large, and more important ... in your life.

After reading Part One you'll have a dramatically new outlook and response to boredom's appearance in your life.

You know that whole thing, "The truth shall set you free"?

Yeah - It's a super-inspiring experience like that. If you pay attention, you'll probably never be bored again (impossible, right?).

But I said this book really isn't about boredom - it's about you.

In Part Two of the book we're going to keep it real and get down to the nitty-gritty.

This won't just be motivational mumbo-jumbo but an actual process ... a how-to of sorts to get you from where you are now to where you want to be (living an awesome life).

At this point you may not even believe an awesome life is possible.

I get that.

So be prepared. We're going to take an intense look at your life. It may get a little heavy. But, growth often, if not always, involves pain and discomfort.

In between some of the chapters I'll be sprinkling in a few pages here and there of "random acts of boredom".

These random thoughts are stories, quotes, or just plain rants about boredom, culture, and you to help give you a new and inspired perspective.

You're going to LOVE the end result of reading this book (If you don't believe me, notice it's in ALL caps, so it must be true, right?).

Are you ready?

You've got this.

Know thy enemy.
Only when you understand boredom's presence in your life can you understand how to defeat it once and for all.

Let's do this.

I Was Bored

I looked out the window, and I just remember being so angry.

Until now, I've never shared this story with anyone. I was too ashamed.

This was before "bored af" even existed as a cultural expression. I was bored af before "bored af" was a thing.

It was a Saturday when I was 16 years old at Valley Forge Military Academy about 800 miles from my home. I loved it there for the most part.

As you could imagine, military school, along with all the sports and extracurricular activities kept me very busy.

But, this particular Saturday, there was nothing on the schedule.

All of my friends on campus were enjoying the weekend, and all of my off-campus friends were busy doing whatever they were doing and somehow I was alone.

This was uncommon for me because I spent a lot of time with teammates and friends being that we all lived on campus together.

I was angry that nobody cared enough about me to invite me to hangout.

It had only been a couple of hours and I felt forgotten.

Shunned.

It wasn't long sitting in that room until I started trying to figure out how people must perceive me to the degree that they didn't want to hang out with me that day.

What kind of nuisance or annoying pest am I?

I mean, the truth was, I had friends galore and a loving support group of people who surrounded me constantly on and off campus. Insomuch that I was always busy, but within just a couple of hours of boredom and loneliness on a Saturday afternoon I started having thoughts I hadn't experienced since I was a child.

"You're worthless," I thought.

"What a pathetic life..."

"Nobody cares about you - you're nothing but a nuisance."

"Just kill yourself and get it over with."

I sat on the desk next to the bunk-bed and cried.

I didn't want to go through with it, but the very fact that I was considering it made me feel like such a loser.

I was bored for one day, and I considered committing suicide.

The truth is, boredom messes with your head.

A Boredom Epiphany

As one of the founding leaders of a student movement, I've been able to watch life unfold for every "kind" of student from nearly every demographic.

I'm always trying to "get to the bottom" of how big life-changing negative things started in a teen or young adult's life.

My work with this age group has revealed a recurring theme that scares me.

I remember when I first had the epiphany.

I began asking more questions to get to the root of the problem. My goal was to determine where the problems started for those that "went down the wrong road".

I figured if I could stop the problem before it started, I can change the course of their lives without a blip on the radar screen.

Here's the story:

It was emotional.

People were crying. A lot of people.

I'd just finished speaking to a crowd of people in a small college town in Illinois.

The response was amazing ... and a little overwhelming.

It wasn't just young students or the kind of people you'd expect to see crying (whatever that means).

It was grown men too with the kind of outward appearance that may cause you to cross the street if you were alone near a dark alley.

I spoke about new beginnings and a fresh start. And apparently a lot of people wanted that.

But, what I said on that day is unimportant.

It was what I learned.

I walked up to one particularly tough looking guy, hoping to learn what he was facing and how he could be helped.

Tears rolled down his cheeks as he told me how he had recently been released from jail.

"You don't know what I've done" he said between sobs. "I've wrecked my life and so many lives besides mine . . . You can't possibly understand."

I believed him.

I hadn't lived his life.

I didn't know his struggle.

I didn't know what he'd done, and I still don't.

But I wanted to know what led him down this path of dysfunction and sorrow to see if there were any clues that may be helpful to the students I lead.

He had the same answers you hear so commonly from a man who had lived a life of crime: Gangs, drugs, poverty, etc . . .

But I pushed further. I was searching for an answer beyond the obvious.

"But, before all of that . . . why'd you get started in that life ... with those people?" I asked. "Where did it all begin?"

You could see his forehead crinkle as he began to wipe some of the tears from his eyes.

It was as if he had never really asked himself the question how his life had taken him to here.

Why had he taken that first fateful step down a path that would lead only to heartache and regret?

After a few seconds of soul searching, I could see the clear answer appear as his eyes widened with discovery.

He looked at me and gave me an answer I had heard many times before in similar situations.

But, I never paid attention.

Foolishly, I would dismiss the answer as a rite of passage and ask more probing questions in pursuit of a "better" answer.

He shrugged his shoulders, looked me in the eye and said, "I was bored."

BORED AF:

A 2-Minute 39-Second Snapshot

Billy's bored.

'Katiee" is so bored she's using suicidal language.

Work didn't solve boredom for Jordan.

'Stubborn' is irritated about being bored.

'Bossmanebobby' is looking for someone to do drugs with to beat the boredom in his life.

Any questions?

BORED AF:

Watch Your Language

You see it everywhere.

On Twitter alone, people express their boredom over 20,000 times a day.

If you haven't written it yourself, you've seen it on social media or in a text from a friend.

It's common.

It's expected. We assume people will get bored.

But, consider what is happening behind the words.

There's a nakedness to you when you express yourself with this level of animus and disgust.

I'm not going to drop the F-Bomb in this book, but look at the language ("AF" stands for "As #@?!").

The intensity in this expression communicates something infinitely more personal than a cultural cliche.

I mean just look at the intense emotion surrounding your use of the word "bored".

It's not just bored af.

It's also "bored as _____" (choose a few other choice vulgarities here) or sooooo bored (notice the emphasis with the elongated "so").

Why? Why does culture - why do we speak of boredom with such strong language?

Answer: Boredom is painful.

CURES THAT DON'T WORK:

Plenty To Do

Society doesn't understand why you're bored.

This is primarily because they believe (and so do you) that boredom is a result of having nothing to do.

You've used the words yourself.

There's nothing to do.

Right?

I mean yeah, there's video games and books and TV shows and music.

There's YouTube and social media and internet sites and entertainment.

There's board games (did he really just use that example?) and hiking and sports and picnic baskets.

But seriously, there's NOTHING to do.

This drives parents and older generations NUTS!

I'm sure you already know this, but if you're reading this book as a teenager and want to make your parents cray-cray, just keep telling them you're bored like every 5 minutes.

Careful though. If you push too far, they may put you to work.

I know it's hard, but imagine a world without internet.

No texting.

Imagine a world where the phones were connected to the wall and you couldn't travel more than 100 feet from your house while on the phone.

If you wanted multiple music selections, you had to carry a walkman and another case with all the additional cd's or even worse cassette tapes of the music you wanted to listen to.

Let's not even discuss the job of fast-forwarding and rewinding those babies.

Sorry, I didn't mean to go all 80's on ya, but that was the world of your parents.

When Nintendo came out and they played Super Mario Brothers or Sonic on Sega, they couldn't do it on a phone.

They couldn't even do it on a cordless controller.

Are you getting the picture?

So, coming from this world, there's EVERYTHING to do.

It is kinda ludicrous to claim there's nothing to do. Because there is.

This is why culture is wrong about the entire boredom discussion.

The truth is there's lots to do. But, you're still bored (and rightfully so).

Here's the deal:

People were bored 100 years ago.

People are bored today.

There was less stuff to do 100 years ago.

There's a lot more stuff to do today.

We've been convinced that entertainment, that "fun stuff to do" is the cure to boredom.

But here we are in a world where everything is accessible. Relationships, communications, creativity, learning, and more are all accessible to everyone at the touch of a button.

You're used to it because you've always lived in it. But most of the world is baffled that people can still be bored.

There's SO MUCH TO DO!!! How can they possibly be bored?

But, they're all wrong.

The cure to boredom is not entertainment.

We're Sure – We're Not Sure

Scientific America, an expert science publication, said the following:

"Easily bored people are at higher risk for depression, anxiety, drug addiction, alcoholism, compulsive gambling, eating disorders, hostility, anger, poor social skills, bad grades and low work   performance.

Despite boredom's ubiquity and pathological associations, psychologists have yet to pin down what, exactly, it is."

I love the part where the smartest people on the planet say, "We're not even sure what it [boredom] is."

But, they know it has a high correlation to many of the issues that just happen to plague young adult culture.

Maybe these scientists are on to something???

I think so.

CURES THAT DON'T WORK:

Tylenol For A Tumor

Boredom is not the problem. Boredom is a symptom.

Like a never ending headache, a symptom alerts a doctor to a potential problem beneath the surface that must be diagnosed before one can truly administer a cure.

A headache can be erased with a Tylenol. But, while you've erased the symptom temporarily the cancer grows uncontested inside.

Society is prescribing a Tylenol for a tumor.

What then is the real disease?

Boredom is the symptom of a visionless life.

You should read that last line at least twice. Think about it.

Can you hear boredom's questioning?

Who are you?

I'm Bored … Again

Nobody gets violently frustrated about something dull that happened one time.

The strong language used when experiencing boredom suggests that it is a regular occurrence.

It is in this frequency, that boredom wreaks its greatest havoc.

The onslaught of boredom.

For something so dull, like water, it wears away at your identity, your personal value of your life.

Boredom tempts you to cheapen yourself.

Like the waves of the sea, it's constant.

In pain, it taunts you with a life void of your highest aspirations. It tempts you to settle for something less - anything that will take away the pain of this moment.

I don't want to be alone … surely if I can just find someone, anyone to talk to me it will take away this unending drudgery of boredom and my sucky life.

@Twitter: "Bored af - someone dm me for pics".

In this continued and regular onslaught of boredom, it is easy to get desperate.

I don't want to feel this way about myself and my circumstance anymore.

How do I rescue myself from the pain of the moment of boredom?

This is what I call the secret place. This is why I've written this book for you.

Here, in the silent moment of boredom, is the proving ground for countless decisions that make you who you are.

People do not become rockstars on the stage. They make themselves a rockstar in the silence of the secret place before the stage lifts them for the world to see.

Who do you want to be?

In the pain of boredom, who have you settled to become?

For my friend in the intro to this book, he settled for an environment that would accept him.

He settled for a gang that would give him community, a lifestyle that would give him a thrill, and a new set of values that celebrated the destruction of others to have their own selfish ends.

Today, the bigger picture haunts him with his fateful decision.

The pain of boredom chased him to a place, an environment, a social network, anything that would alleviate the pain and meaningless of a boring existence. Drugs, whatever - anything to find identity outside of being bored.

He didn't set out to be that kind of guy. But, by his own recognition, it was a slow march from the secret place we call bored.

Go Jump Out Of A Plane

I don't think you believe me yet.

But, seeking out entertainment to beat boredom is even worse than I suggested in the last chapters.

I mean, if someone asked you to do something really fun and exciting right now like go see your favorite band backstage or go skydiving, you wouldn't be bored, right?

And, you can think of lots of times that you did something really fun and weren't bored.

So, why shouldn't you seek out those experiences again or experiences like that to beat boredom in your life?

Seriously, if you get to do awesome stuff, go for it.

Do it as often as possible.

I'm just saying it's like food. Once you consume it, you're always going to need more.

Plus, once you've done a lot of awesome stuff, other things lose their *wow* factor.

I did something terrible once.

Unfortunately, I can never undo it.

I learned to cook.

Before that, all I could cook was Ramen Noodles and Frozen Pizza. But, I started watching Gordon Ramsey cuss everyone out on TV and make these dishes that looked super-yummy.

I jumped on YouTube and started working along with him to make pure awesomeness for my mouth.

You should come over and try my pork chops someday. HOLLER!

Anyways, one BIG problem.

Now, I cannot eat a lot of people's food. It's just not good, at all.

Before that, I could eat ramen noodles and be like "hmmmmm".
But, I've elevated my palette, and it ruined me. Big Mac? I might as well eat a pair of smelly socks.

When you have great experiences, the same things happen to you.

Everything else pales in comparison.

Awesomeness elevates your experiential taste buds, and now, it's harder to compete to find pleasure in something that, yes … can be entertaining.

Just like a smelly sock Big Mac can satisfy the hunger, the random activity can still fill the time, but it cannot fill the longing in your soul for more.

Wow. Super poetic, right?!

But, seriously. Even though you can point to awesome experiences where you were never bored, this only increases the likelihood that you'll be bored the next day.

Like staring at a fridge and pantry crammed with food and saying there's nothing to eat.

It's time you understand that twinkie experiences won't satisfy the cravings of the inner person.

You. Want. More.

More as in quality, not as in quantity.

Looking for the next great experience to fill the void and cure boredom is like a junky searching for the next high.

You're a fiend in a cycle.

Drugs don't eliminate the pain. They don't solve a problem.

They provide nothing but an escape. But, soon enough, you crash.

Reality returns and you have one choice. Hustle for another high or deal with the reality staring you in the face.

In student culture today, parents and friends are the pushers and the students are the fiends, jonesing for another experience to beat back the boredom.

But how do we end the vicious cycle?

CULTURAL CONSIDERATIONS:

Bored Blunts

I wonder how much of the party scene is less about a run to fun and more about a run from the pain of boredom.

Boredom forces us to ask the question who we are.

I'm not sure why, but it seems we seek for identity only in reflections.

Boredom's frequency and constant prodding tempts us to find that reflection somewhere, anywhere.

The party scene makes it easy.

@Twitter: Bored af. Who wants to get lit?

In the crowded room, we know that some are there simply to escape the pain of something in their lives.

For some, it's abuse and dysfunction. Broken families. For some, it's the lonely question and boredom's temptation, "Who Am I?"

With one hit, one snort, many find the cheer of the crowd, plus the elation of a temporary high more than adequate to escape from the drudgery of boredom's prodding.

With nothing to do that makes us feel alive, elated, and accepted, the party scene becomes a clear choice for the lost soul with no identity, other than that which is now reflected in the mirror of present company.

Let's just have fun. Let's party.

The Most Important Quote In This Book

"Boredom is a vital problem for moralists since half the sins of mankind are caused by the fear of it."

- Bertrand Russell British Philosopher and Social Critic

When you run away from boredom, what do you run towards?

Rebel Without A Cause

Maybe I'm pushing it too far, but it seems to me the person who is bored, below the surface, is expressing frustration with a society who tolerates boredom as a regular part of everyday life.

Or maybe it's a frustration that somehow your life has fallen victim to its drudgery.

Deep inside of you, I think you know (or at least wish it was true) that boredom should neither be expected nor tolerated.

I agree.

Making A Name For Yourself

BANG.

We don't know for sure, but the 22-year-old college baseball player probably heard the sound of the gunshot a split second after the bullet ripped into his body.

Lying on the ground bleeding out is where Christopher Lane would take his final breath.

A Black Ford Focus with a white sticker in the back window sped away. Luckily, a neighbor saw the car.

Michael Jones, 17, was driving the car. James Edwards, 15, was seated in the back seat and Chancey Luna took the shot.

Police would apprehend all three within hours.

When questioned, it was the 17-year-old that explained why they killed him.

They didn't know Chris Lane, but they saw him jog by the house.

Jones said, "We were bored and didn't have anything to do, so we decided to kill somebody."

Later, investigators would explain to the world that these bored teens were "trying to make a name for themselves."

CURES THAT DON'T WORK:

Isn't This Normal?

The cure to boredom is vision.

Put another way, the single biggest problem facing student and young adult culture today is one of identity.

As I was writing this book, someone asked me, "Isn't that the natural struggle and maturation of that age group though? They're trying to figure out who they are, right?"

"Yes, but they're delaying," I said.

"Pop culture's solutions have trained them to wait until tomorrow. Have fun today ... you're young. And so they chase fun, entertainment, busyness, and wait."

But your soul is screaming out to be something real and lasting.

A large part of culture's dysfunction exists in and because of the delay.

STOP IT.

Incalculable Damages

The ramifications of boredom extends far beyond the oft-mentioned issues of young adults "on the fringes" or "troubled".

Consider the girl who is well-liked, gets excellent grades, and is popular.

School comes easy to her. She's active in extracurricular activities, but she's still bored.

For her, everything is after. After school, after college, after a few years in that new career.

Culture's message of tomorrow makes her bored with her today.

And so, in boredom, she waits. 5-10 years...Enduring the drudgery of the mundane in hopes of meaningful impact in the unknown tomorrow.

But where does that leave her today?

Equally important where does that leave the world?

It leaves her enduring a nightmare present and the world un-touched by her gifts, today.

Just have fun - you're still young.

What lives could have been touched?

What companies could have been started?

What meaningful contribution could have been made by her?

Maybe <u>success</u> is fun to her!

Maybe she has an idea Right Now!

But, in boredom, the world tells her to watch another show, find some friends, or add another extracurricular activity.

I don't know how many lives have been destroyed by someone who ran to the vices of culture to hide away the pain.

But, the opportunity lost... The incalculable damage of those who, in boredom procrastinated their gifts' release to the world, I'm sure, is even more staggering.

Boredom is alerting you to a candle hid in a bush. It's speaking in your spirit.

But, we've treated boredom's call to arms, its invitation to take our place in the world, with the devil's most effective strategic weapon - delay.

The Alarm Clock

Boredom is defined as a state of being weary and restless through lack of interest.

But, I guess I'm asking what it is beyond its definition.

From a spiritual perspective, what is boredom's role in your life? (Woah - I got deep quick, right?!)

I believe boredom is an alarm clock.

It's only role in life is meant to wake you up at exactly the right time.

We say Dreams are made in the night, but are they?

T.E. Lawrence said famously,

"All men dream, but not equally
Those who dream by night in the dusty recesses of their minds wake up in the day to find it was vanity
But the dreamers of the day are dangerous men, for they act their dreams with open eyes, to make it possible."

What if boredom is nothing more than the alarm to wake you from the slumber of the mundane?

Vanity reigns. AWAKE!!!

Does boredom tug at the sheets of a life void of its true ability.

Is boredom's nuisance a whisper in your ear that says "Wake up. You were made for more."

Is that nagging frustration with boredom's voice, the sleep of a sluggard experiencing a nightmare not intended to be your life's reality?

Is it possible boredom's siren sound evokes such emotion because it alerts you to another world – a world in which you're called to dream with open eyes?

Either You Know Or
You Don't Know

Perhaps boredom's unwelcomed interruption is for one of two reasons: You know, or you don't know.

What do I know you ask?

Yourself.

You know you've got something. Something that who dream in the day, those who awake to act and mold reality into a creation of their own making.

If "you know," that's you. And you know it.

Boredom shrieks its dull prodding nuisance to awaken you to a new reality of your own making.

Your response?

[The snooze button] - "@twitter bored af. someone dm me for
_____. Hmu"

[The snooze button] - porn.
[The snooze button] - binge watching Netflix.

[The snooze button] - movies anyone?
[The snooze button] - anyone wanna hit a blunt?

You delay your destiny.

It's time to take your stage in the world boredom cries.
[snooze button]

A little sleep a little slumber a little folding of the hands to sleep.

Awaken to your possibilities - now is the moment! This is your time! [snooze button]

So shall your poverty come and your want as an armed man.

Why you ask can't I do _____? I just wish I could...

"If only" are the cries of one mumbling in his sleep.

Boredom alerts you to the reality of your identity outside of the pain of your currently experienced reality.

But it doesn't seem real. Not possible. The fear of what if... the questions about a world we've yet to truly experience delay us from accepting boredoms call to awaken and experience it in its fullness.

But I'm begging you to accept boredom's gift and function in your life.

I implore you to take your hand off the snooze button of delay and dysfunction to hide the pain of a present nightmare world and a dull existence.

Boredom cries AWAKEN & ARISE.

To what you yell. Why should I wake? Awake to what?

Your potential. Your purpose. A world of your own creation.

I invite you to awaken to another dream. An epic journey. To a fight, a battleground, and a world where you are the hero.

Fighting valiantly for something meaningful, join the story where you are the central character in an epic fight for good... A dream world that - a true reality where potential is actualized.

Hear boredom's siren sound. Accept its gift and function in your life.

This is your moment.

It's your time.

But, what about if you don't know?

You don't know your value (Most people don't).

What do you do?

Who are you?

PART TWO

I am NOT going to give you four steps to beating boredom and living an awesome life in this section. I'm going to give you four ingredients.

Here's the difference: Steps are sequential, but ingredients can be in any order.

So here are the four ingredients to an awesome life now. Enjoy the concoction!

1. Dream
2. Explore/Learn
3. Collaborate
4. Create

Dreams & Visions

In college, as a Philosophy major, I had to read lots of weird stuff, including prophets from thousands of years ago.

I read Nostradamus, and Greek mythology, and religious passages from countless ancient sources.

But the following ancient passage has stayed special to me.

"And afterward, I will pour out my Spirit on all people. Your sons and daughters will prophesy, your old men will dream dreams, your young men will see visions...

I will show wonders in the heavens and on the earth, blood and fire and billows of smoke. The sun will be turned to darkness and the moon to blood before the coming of the great and dreadful day"

Thousands of years ago, in a moment that would decide the fate of countless men and women, a prophet spoke these words of impending doom upon his nation.

Like many of the ancient prophets, many of his weird prophecies have actually happened, but some have not...yet (Thankfully).

This prophecy has always stuck with me.

It points to something they understood even thousands of years ago, something deep, that can help you start living in awesomeness now.

Notice that the context of his prophecy is a pretty messed up world. Cataclysmic type stuff (Extra points for the biggest word in the whole book).

Before he writes the post above, he tells of a coming army that will destroy their nation and goes into graphic detail about the opposing army's destructive power over them.

It's an epic moment.

Here's why I'm sharing this ancient text: I'm amazed at what the Hebrew prophet promises their God will do to rescue them.

To a nation in the midst of complete and utter destruction, God promises to give them dreams and visions.

He offers to show them a world that does not yet exist, but could exist.

The expectation seems to be that:

If only their God will give dreams and visions ...

If they can just see the possibilities of another world...

Even if the "real world" is all messed up and virtually destroyed...

The prophecy suggests the dreamers will rise up and recreate the world they experience in their dreams, but is not yet their reality!

But, it all begins by receiving a dream.

It begins with a dream for you too.

DREAM

So, here's the cure.

I want to help you beat boredom once and for all in your life.

There's no pill, but conquering boredom may be the most ex-hilarating life adventure ever.

Now before I give you the cure, I want to say that it may seem a little corny at first.

But, I've watched. I've seen it in my own life too.

This works.

If boredom is a symptom of a visionless life, the real issue that must be treated is vision.

This is not vision as in your eyesight.

This is vision as in, the first and most important part to con-quering boredom and living an awesome life is to dream.

That's right. Dream.

Dream with your eyes open.

BIGGER

So, the first step of the cure is pretty simple.

If you're anything like the students or young adults in the movement I serve, you hear what to do, but you don't <u>really</u> hear it.

"Yeah. Yeah. Got it. Dream."

This is going to help you think through some things that have been roadblocks to you being your best.

When I tell most people to dream, to think about the life they want to live, they think within the limitations of their experience or maybe just a little bit bigger.

For example, if I'm talking to a student and his family has been in a constant cycle of drug use, addiction, and drug dealing, his dream will be just outside of those bounds.

"I don't wanna live in the drama of my parents and family getting arrested and getting high all the time. I like cars, so if I could get a job paying like $25 an hour and never live in the mess my family lives... that'd be perfect."

Notice, he didn't say he wanted to cure cancer or create the next multi-billion dollar tech startup.

Why?

I've had so many of these exact kinds of conversations.

The answer is so often the same.

I'd ask "Why not start the next billion dollar car startup or create a cure to cancer?"

He'd say, "That's not me man. I can't."

Please listen to me. Please!!!

I HATE THAT ANSWER!!!

But, I think I know why it's so commonly expressed.

I call it the "finding yourself fallacy."

The Finding Yourself Fallacy

Somewhere in the plethora of media and in the hodgepodge of cultural conversation, we've come to believe in this idea of "finding yourself."

I get it.

I hear the cultural influencers and celebrities pounding the pulpit of a religion that says, "Just. Be. You."

And to a degree, I agree.

Be yourself.

But this begs the real question.

(Get ready I'm about to go deep here).

Who are you?

More importantly, when you "be you," what does the concept of "youness" really entail?

(I told you it would get deep). Read the above ^ line again.

Let me break it down by talking about your potential.

Remember in grade school when your teacher would sit down with your parents and talk about whether you were "working to your potential"?

This idea of "potential" suggested limits.

It makes us think of potential like we would think of a cup.

It may be a big cup or a small cup, but it can only hold so much liquid.

The idea of potential was the same, "<u>You</u>" had <u>potential</u>. There are and were limitations to your capacity.

How much you could do, how smart you could be, what grades you could get, etc ...

So, if you think of your "youness" like that, like a cup with limitations, being "yourself" is limited to what you've already seen done or done yourself. Maybe just a little bit more you believe you can do with the extra effort to complete your potential.

AND SO!!!!

When culture screams "Be yourself", you limit your capacity for greater possibilities based on a belief in a "youness" of limited capacity and potential.

However, this limited capacity of "youness" you've come to believe in is a complete sham and a bold faced lie that can destroy your life!!!

While there is certainly some limit to a human's capacity, the idea that you've come anywhere close to the <u>best</u> you can be is asinine!

The Finding Yourself Fallacy (Part 2)

Let's say you start improving yourself in one area that you enjoy or find meaningful.

You work at it and learn a new way to do it that gives you a better result with less effort.

This "learning" you experienced just multiplied your potential. Do you see it?

For example, you learn if you do something in a different sequential order, it makes the process twice as fast.

By learning that, your capacity or potential you had before you learned that has grown to a greater capacity due to that new-found capability.

This improvement opens up new possibilities, possibilities that were not accounted for when you first measured your "potential".

Then, you have to account for your creative ability.

By focusing on an issue or problem, you may create an entirely new solution that has unexpected benefits. This creation makes the world different and changes the possibilities entirely.

But, wait ... you don't have to do it alone. You decide to bring in other people.

You show this new sequence or creation to a couple of friends who are working the project with you and now you have access to their capacity for their creativity and added ideas all making the process better and increasing potential.

Why?

Because potential is ever increasing.

Every time you learn something, every time you bring someone else in, every time you create a new idea, this allows for ever expanding potential.

So... the truth is, to a very high degree, the word potential is meaningless.

It's not a static unmoving category.

It's not a limitation of who you are because every time you learn, create, or collaborate your potential multiplies.

Potential is for the most part, meaningless, because your capacity for greatness in truth is not limited. It is, for all intents and purposes, unlimited.

So potential is not real, and a limited you... an idea that I am not enough is meaningless as well.

Because as you grow and as you become better and as you collaborate and as you move towards a vision that is bigger than you potential will grow and " youness" will change.

There is no static "you" that you're called to find.

You are called to find a vision.

You're called to find a fight that matters.

You're called to find a place in which you can thrive, but "you" as a limitation, you will never find.

And please don't try. Because that you is boring.

The Artist

For example, what if you were good at art? You enjoy the fun of it.

Then you learn a new way to test which of your artistic projects are most likely to get attention and be purchased.

This allows for you to give more of your time and effort into your creative passion because now it is profitable.

Your extra time improving your art skills results in you creating even more exceptional art.

One day, you are talking with a friend about your art and learn that he is very good at spreading the word and marketing.

He offers to sell your artwork for a percentage of the profits.

You learn that there are lots of people like your friend who help good artists sell their work.

You decide to hire five more marketers who you only pay when they sell your art.

Through this initial collaboration, you have learned, which grew your potential.

You took action and now have a whole team working to sell your art while you focus on creating it.

Notice that your art may have started in a garage, but you learned and your potential grew. You collaborated with someone who had different gifts and your potential and impact grew even more.

Then, you used what you learned from hiring one person and multiplied it to a whole team of people.

By choosing to create, by choosing to collaborate, and by choosing to explore new possibilities your potential has now grown exponentially.

All you really need to do is choose. Choose to create. Chose to explore and learn. Choose to collaborate.

All things are possible.

You Can Do Anything You Want

When I was a teenager, my mentor told me, "You can do anything you want."

I wish I would have believed him.

I thought I did, but I didn't really.

Let me tell you something.

You can do anything you want.

You may think you believe me, but you don't.

End the cycle of self-imposed limitations.

Believe me.

Questions

Anything you want to do is possible.

Here's a few simple questions you could ask yourself to start exploring down the right roads:

What did you dream about doing as a kid?

If I gave you 1 Billion Dollars, what would you do with it (Besides throwing a huge party and blowing it all on your houses and cars- that gets boring fast)?

If I could wave a magic wand and you could do anything you wanted, what would you do?

What's the one thing I can do in my life right now such that by doing it everything else becomes easier or unnecessary?

What angers you? What injustice or wrong should stop? What needs to be done to change it?

The answer to any one or all of these questions are worth exploring. If the answer inspires you and you take action, bold and passionate action, you've found yourself.

Now look in the mirror.

Do you like who you see?

Are you inspired?

EVEN BIGGER

The idea of unlimited human potential is certainly inspiring, but it gets better for you.

"You are living in the most extraordinary time in human history." - Billionaire and Technologist Peter Diamandis

While human potential is unlimited, I think it's safe to say that it's far easier to build a skyscraper today than it would have been 1,000 years ago.

Why am I saying this? Because this idea of a "you" of limited capacity has GOT to go!

Open your eyes to the possibilities that YOU, yes YOU are capable of accomplishing!

The road has been paved in advance.

Many of the obstacles are already removed.

Anything you are curious enough or passionate enough to pursue is accessible unlike any time ever before.

Anything.

Peter Diamandis is currently running 17 companies, one of which is working on mining asteroids of their precious metals as they fly past earth!

Yeah.

But, it's not just him pushing the limits of human capabilities.

It's the young. It's the Snapchat creators, the Facebook founders, the start-up ventures both for-profit and not, and more.

15-year-olds are finding fresh approaches to diagnosing cancer faster than any tests of the past. They're starting 4 and 5-star restaurants at 16 years-old.

It's becoming a regular phenomenon.

How is that possible?

It's all possible now.

And that's the point.

Opportunity Of A Lifetime

I could write 10 books on the possibilities sitting in front of you.

But the problem is no longer the possibilities.

The problem is one of belief.

The problem is one of choice.

People used to say (and some erroneously still do), "Opportunity only knocks once."

They couldn't be more wrong.

The challenge is no longer finding an opportunity.

The big challenge is deciding which opportunity to pursue.

It's Never Over – The Best You Ever

You're always in pursuit of your best self.

And, it's in that pursuit, that your identity is whole and alive.

If you're anything like me, you just want to arrive. You want to be the perfect you.

I like one Ancient Greek version of the word "perfect". It does not mean without flaw. It means whole or complete for its stage in maturity.

The warrior is not great only as he stands on the conquered hill of victory. The warrior is great in the battle, fighting and pursuing an aim that is honorable and worthy of his life's investment ... even his entire life if necessary.

Win or lose, live or die, it was not the accolades or the medals at the end of the battle that made that warrior great. It was the pursuit of excellence, the commitment to a worthy cause, and the faithful execution of a life spent in preparation that performed when it counted ... on the battlefield, as he fought for a cause bigger than himself.

Here's the problem. If you're bored, you're not pursuing anything.

You're waiting.

You're contemplating.

You're dreaming with closed eyes about doing something worthy, but you've failed to invest yourself.

To open your eyes.

To commit.

To decide.

And then to take action.

Your boredom is communicating to you that you're ready for the next level.

So go.

You Can't Do Anything

You can do anything.

Okay, confession here.

I can't sing. I asked my Grammy-Nominated friend who can both sing (obviously) and dance if I could learn to sing. (And yes, bragging about a Grammy-nominated friend is really awesome)

Anyways, he said "yes", I think anyone could learn.

I'm still doubtful. Despite my tries to sing, I probably still sound more like someone strangling a cat when I try to hit the high notes.

My point is, I can't do anything.

I'm guessing that feels like a total contradiction to my title cuz I did kinda say you can do anything…. and then I said, I can't….

So, here's the deal. When people say you can do anything, and then you try to do something and you can't… that tends to be disheartening and you'll question the authenticity (or intelligence) of the person who said you could do anything.

Right?

I mean motivational hype is nice and may give you goosebumps, but if it's just a fiction, that's a total downer.

Saying "You can do anything" is not suggesting you can shoot lasers out of your eyes or grow metal claws out of your hands.

You're not an X-Man or a superhero.

You can do anything in the realm of possibility, although don't limit yourself because we live in an age that is pushing the envelope of possibility far past anything anyone thought possible.

So, I wanna settle this whole "You can do anything" dilemma forever.

When I say "You can do anything", I mean you can do anything you'd truly want to do.

Gifts & Callings

This is a really important part to this whole boredom beating thing and awesome life living.

The truth is, people don't like doing things they're not good at.

You are gifted.

Unfortunately, society has stolen that word and, in many cases, limited "gifted" to the context of academic achievement.

That's not what I'm saying.

I'm saying you're born with certain natural innate abilities to which you'll naturally and easily excel.

Some would argue that you get good at whatever you choose to work at. (The whole nature vs nurture discussion).

I agree you get better at whatever you work at.

But, no matter how hard I work at singing, I'll never be better than my naturally gifted Grammy-Nominated singing friend.

Why?

That's not my gift.

Here's what that doesn't mean! Just because I have a gift doesn't mean I do not have to work at getting better at it.

There are plenty of gifted but lazy people who peak at a much better than average level of their gift, but are never truly great because they don't nurture their nature.

As I heard Presidential Candidate Carly Fiorina once say, "What you are is God's gift to you and what you make of yourself is your gift to God."

Drop the mic, Carly. Drop. The. Mic.

Not Gifted – I Suck

When I talk about gifting, a couple of responses are common.

"I want to be gifted at _____, but I suck."

It seems like everybody wants to be the cool rockstar or athlete. The money ain't bad either!

Two Quick Facts about sucking:

1- If you're young (say under 25), in many cases, I've found you don't know if you suck or not.

In a book called "Multipliers" by Liz Wiseman, she points out that sometimes we are amazing at something and assume that everyone else can do it as well as us and as easy as us, but it's not the case. It's a gift you don't recognize.

Then, there's other examples like Michael Jordan who couldn't make the JV team as a Freshman in high school.

Again, gifted does not necessarily mean you are better than everyone else or that you do not need to work to develop your skills.

I was a terrible speaker as a teenager, but I loved doing it and was brave enough to get onstage.

I REALLY wanted to do it.

That's the key. Because I REALLY wanted to speak well, I enjoyed working at it. I still do.

So, what's the point? If you wish you could do something, but suck, it may be too early for you to determine your gifting.

This leads me to the second important point.

2- Sometimes, if not always, you'll find your gift while pursuing a different interest.

For example, all through high school and college I was convinced I wanted to be an attorney.

In that pursuit, I learned to write better in preparation for law school.

I also saw myself standing and speaking to juries in court. So, I grew more and more adept at speaking.

I never went to law school, and I'm glad I didn't.

I later learned it wasn't law school I wanted - law school was simply as BIG as I was capable of dreaming at that time.

But, I learned my gifts in the process of exploring and diligently working towards a dream and a vision for my life.

You will too.

So don't be discouraged!

Giftless

This leads me to the second common response I hear to the gifting/calling discussion!

"I don't have any gifts."

Maybe you don't feel like you're naturally good at anything.

You may say, "That's not me."

Why can't it be you?

I want to rebuke you.

I want to bring a group of your friends into the room so they can tell you what you're good at.

I wish I could get in your face. I wish I could do an intervention. I wish I could make you cry with fresh understanding of your capability.

But, this is a book... so I can't.

So let's assume you're right.

You're not good at anything. (I hated to write that lie, but it's your lie, and you believe it, so I want to deal with it so you can live in awesomesauce.)

If someone were actually not good at anything, I'd say to stop being boring.

Harsh? That's not my intent. You'll see what I mean.

I'm Boring

A counselor I know had a son who would always mix up his usage of his words.

It was so cute!

One day, he said to his Mom, "Mom, I'm boring."

He meant to say "I'm bored".

Without hesitation, his Mom said, "That's right, but if you'll stop being boring, you'll stop being bored."

Think about it.

Exploration

The key to finding your identity is not to look at the reflections from what you've done... especially the reflection looking back as you delayed your destiny.

That reflection may be good or bad... probably a little of both.

It's time to explore a new alternative.

"Finding yourself" is not a search for a static and unchanging mystery you.

"Finding yourself" is a matter of exploring all the world has to offer and pursuing your best self as you contribute to those things that inspire you and that you find, through exploration, that you love.

If you don't explore the possibilities, how will you know what you're gifting is?

That's the next step.

Now that you know you'll find yourself in the journey towards the dream, you only have one job - Explore.

Curiosity

"The cure for boredom is curiosity. There is no cure for curiosity." - Ellen Parr

Still Stuck?

If the 5 questions in the Dreaming chapter didn't inspire you but instead filled your head with doubt, you only have one option: Explore.

It's not uncommon. Often those of you who are a "realist" (or maybe, just maybe a "pessimist") don't like to think in dream worlds that have no resemblance to reality.

But, if you cannot dream of doing something exceptional, the only thing you can do is actually experience something exceptional yourself.

As part of our student movement, we help facilitate this with what we call "CTW Teams" (CTW stands for Change the World).

When we think about changing the world, we think about the basic pillars or spheres of influence that sociologists look to as the basic building blocks of civilized culture.

Take a look at each of them and see which interests you most...

Arts & Entertainment (celebrities)
Religion (spiritual leaders)

Education (teachers)
Government (politicians)
Family
Media (Influencers)
Business (Startups, CEO's, and Billionaires)

Which do you think could best help you change an issue important to you?

If none of those interest you, is there anything you see in the world that angers or frustrates you?

Here are a couple to look at:

- Not having enough money/poverty
- Spiritual dysfunction or spiritual ignorance
- People who don't have access to good education
- Idiot politicians ruining lives
- Dysfunctional homes/families
- Orphans
- Domestic abuse
- Getting the word out about important issues/having a voice
- Just plain helping people have a good time

Then there's issues like:

- Depression
- Bullying
- The party scene
- Gang violence
- Cutting
- Sexual slavery/trafficking
- etc...

Pick one... or two.

Whatever grabs your attention.
If nothing grabs your attention - pick two anyways.

Flip a coin - make it one.

If it's issue specific, Google a local group trying to affect the issue you care about (or just hit us up at the 99 movement - we need lots of help with lots of different issues).

If it's a category that interests you, pick a category and an issue.

Now call a local group working to impact the issue that interests you.

Tell them, "I'd love to help you accomplish your mission."

Who there is in charge of (name your category)?

I'd love to help.

It doesn't have to be non-profit either.

Call a company and ask to work for free until you prove your worth.

Or, better yet, start your own company.

Or buy one (Raise the money if you don't have any).

Don't have enough experience? Find a partner who does!

You used to need permission. Status.

But now, you can find the missing pieces you need easier than ever. The knowledge, the people, the capital ... it's all looking for someone with vision.

You can do anything you want. Just decide!

Your Best – Your Duty

According to old news reports, the ship called "Lady Elgin" collided with another ship called the Augusta in the ice cold waters of Lake Michigan sometime not long after 2 AM.

Of the 300 passengers, many drowned immediately. Others grabbed onto the wreckage of the ship hoping for a rescue late into the night.

The Lake was rough with large crashing waves and a fierce undertow. Many times, even the passengers getting close to shore on the wreckage were beaten by the waves and sucked back out to sea by the current.

This was the scene that Edward Spence happened upon as he walked late into the night and looked out to the cold waters of Lake Michigan.

Being an experienced swimmer, Edward tied a rope to his body and swam through the cold rough waters to a victim clutching a piece of the wreckage.

His friends on the shore would then grab the rope and pull them back in as the waves beat their bodies into the wreckage and rough terrain of the shore.

Unwilling to give up, after each rescue, Edward would bravely rush back to the treacherous waters to reach another of the countless victims begging his help.

After SIX hours through the night, bruised, scraped, and exhausted by his fight against the sea Edward passed out on the shore.

Edward saved 17 lives on that fateful night.

He woke up in his room in Evanston to his brother Will looking over him.

His first words were, "Will, did I do my full duty ... Did I do my best?"

Years later, Will would tell people that Edward never recovered from that experience.

"His face would turn Ashen pale, and Edward would ask, 'Tell me the truth. Did I fail to do my best?'"

Maybe I've seen too much of the pain and brokenness of the young adult culture. But I see a world in need of rescuing.

In each of the issues that plague our culture, ranging from human trafficking to the victims of abuse on various levels, I see people clinging to the wreckage of a life filled with dysfunction.

The world needs your help.

Don't be bored. Be your best.

So Easy A 10-Year-Old Can Do It

So, let me introduce you to Emily. She's 10.

Emily learned that she loved having sleepovers. Big surprise for a 10-year-old girl, right?

So, she did what any 21st century 10-year-old would do, she decided to start putting together AMAZING sleepovers for her friends.

She would work with her Mom to plan them out and invite her friends over for the fun.

Now that they're amazing sleepovers, she does the next obvious step - SHOW THE WORLD! She's on YouTube.

She decided to teach more girls how to have awesome sleepovers so her channel is working on creating weekly videos to have a perfectly themed sleepover every month of the year.

But, now she needs money for video equipment, editors, supplies, etc ...

So, she convinced a local pizza place to let her sell pizza cards that give people discounts and free pizzas.

She's raised over $5,000 at an average of around $90 an hour. It only took her a few months. Not too shabby.

Now she's turning the enterprise into a business where busy Mom's can buy the Sleepover in a box so they don't have to recreate or go shopping for all the games and supplies.

Hmmm...

How should she get the word out?

She's writing a book. It's called "5 Steps To The Perfect Sleepover". She sells the book to Mom's and Aunt's and Uncle's who buy it for the little girls in their lives that they love.

The girls will see the book and go to YouTube and watch the show and hopefully, beg their parents to have that awesome sleepover.

Emily is excited. Why? She's getting paid to do AWESOME sleepovers AND she takes a percentage of the money and is supporting orphans in foreign countries.

Yeah...

Now, what's the point?

Emily explored and found something she loved.

She didn't know how to be a YouTube star, a videographer, a marketer, a salesperson, an author, or a philanthropist.

But now she is.

How?

She decided to become all of those things as she explored a possibility she loved.

And it's just the beginning for her, and for you too.

Now get going!!!!

P.S. - Emily is my daughter. #HumbleBrag

The Youngest Self-Made Billionaire

Elizabeth Holmes dropped out of college at 19 and revolution-ized the way blood tests were done.

She wasn't a doctor or even a nurse.

Now, at 30, she is the youngest self-made female billionaire on the planet.

Was she a genius or did she just find a problem she wanted to solve and go after it?

In a CNN Money magazine interview she said, ""I think a lot of young people have incredible ideas and incredible insights, but sometimes they wait before they go give their life to some-thing. What I did was just to start a little earlier."

Give your life to something.

Start earlier.

Dating Not Married

Around Junior and Senior year of high school students start stressing out about what are HUGE life decisions.

Which college?

Which profession?

Once in college, I think the average college student changes their major like 5 times.

After getting out, many Millennials are struggling to find work in the context of the major they've chosen!

Trying to make a decision about profession or life's work in either high school or college made sense even twenty years ago, but no more.

I think some are paralyzed by the decision. Give it a rest - you probably do not know 100% exactly what you want to spend the rest of your life doing!

Committing to a life-plan at a young age - totally unnecessary.
Think about your pursuit for your best self as dating, not marriage.

Stop stressing! You don't have to choose for life anymore.

But, didn't the last chapter just say, "Give your life to something?"

Yes, but not for life ... unless you want to.

Collaboration

Don't do dreams alone.

You're stronger together.

Collaboration exponentially increases potential.

If you have good friends, that makes this step on your journey even easier.

Now that you've done the work of exploration for a dream, you should have something to give your life to... At least for a month or so...

Sense you don't know it all, and don't want to waste your time learning everything, find people who already know.

For example, if you decide you love music and want to do a benefit concert for victims of cutting and self-harm, you know you're going to need some spectacular visuals for concert posters.

A YouTube video announcing the concert to share on social media might help too!

So, start telling everyone what you're doing. Go to the school AV club and find people who like doing video who want some publicity.

Talk to artists and ask them to help.

Set up a meeting at your house, or the local coffee place... Whatever. Get 2 to 3 people on board to help.

Figure out what else you need.

Tell the others to help you find more help.

Make some super organized person the project manager.

Guess what you're doing?

You've started a movement.

Find someone to tell the story of self abuse.

Tell everyone the story.

Talk about solutions.

Raise money.

Raise awareness.

Now look in the mirror.

See your reflection?

It only gets better... And harder.

But it's worth it.

PS – you inspire me. Now, go do it again...

PSS - starting a movement too hard? Join a movement already in progress!

God, Eyes, And Reflections

My 8-year old, Alex, always asks the deepest questions.

I'm jealous.

Once he asked me, "Daddy, why did God make us so that we cannot see ourselves?"

Yeah ... try answering that one!

We only see ourselves in reflections.

That's true of not just your physical reflection, but you.

It's only in the reflection of someone else's eyes that we truly come to know ourselves.

We look to the world to tell us who we are or at least confirm our suspicions.

Perhaps that's why we crave acceptance.

We only really know we're valuable if someone tells us.

Can we only see ourselves (or our possible selves) in the value we bring to others?

Maybe this was intentional from our creator. Selfishness is not the way. Our value and worth comes in our ability to serve and give value to another, not merely ourselves.

This is why your friends are the single best indicator of the kind of person you have decided to be.

What your friends value or find important will be reflected in you or else, they will not find you "valuable" and they would not be friends with you.

As I've expressed, when you're bored, you explore and experiment with things you otherwise may not have.

The hope is finding joy and acceptance in the reflection from the crowd.

This is dangerous because they may celebrate that which is destructive to you and your life's purpose.

Plus, the crowd is fickle.

Don't settle for a group that accepts you. Find people that inspire you.

If what they value is good and worthy of your investment, it's in their reflection that you finally see yourself in the best light.

Do your friends inspire you?

Who have they told you that you are?

More Friends

You can see it so clearly on social media.

"dm me for pics."

"Somebody talk to me, I'm bored."

"Lms and I'll tell u the truth."

It's perfectly natural. We find meaning or at least solace in community.

Social media and texting provide the perfect avenues to excuse our boredom with thoughts like:

At least I'm not the only one that's bored.

Or

If somebody hits me up, at least I know they're there for me.

But have you ever been bored while with someone?

I assume the answer is yes.

Do you hear what I'm saying?

It's completely possible to be bored together.

So, while boredom plays particular tricks on the mind while alone, boredom can exist in community.

Friends are NOT a boredom cure. In most cases, I'm guessing you're looking to friends in hopes to find fun together, which is great.

But having fun with friends together is a similar attempt to using entertainment to cure the boredom yourself.

Eventually, the friends will leave. And you'll still be bored and alone.

Even if they stayed forever, eventually you'd get bored ... with them (interpret that any way you want).

Bored Sex

I woke up to my college roommate losing his virginity.

Awkward?

Yes.

He never knew I knew.

The weird thing was a few days before we had talked about the fact that he wanted to wait for someone special... the one, ya know?

But, I woke up to hear her pressuring him into it.

It was too awkward to say anything, and I couldn't see them (thank God).

Their relationship was a non-starter.

I was sad for him. He lost his virginity to a one-night stand.

He seemed really depressed the following week.

I wonder how many people settle.

You know what I mean?

It goes down something like this.

You're bored, and tired of not being in a relationship. You're invited to a party. He/She show you some attention.

Any other time, you would've never given them the time of day.

But, you're bored.

So, you start hanging with someone who doesn't inspire you.

But, they're fun... you're enjoying the cat and mouse of chasing each other and you're no longer bored... you laugh more.

So you settle. You start hooking up.

I'm going to say something controversial here...

But, I have to say it.

Countless times, I've witnessed first-hand the destructive power a sexual relationship has on people's lives.

Hollywood and the entertainment industry in the same breath wants to worship the power and intimacy of the sexual relationship and AT THE SAME TIME dismiss the casual sexual encounter as nothing to even worry about.

Fact: You can't have it both ways!

Either it's a beautiful, intimate, and spiritual bonding of two people or it's a raw emotionless evolutionary perfunctory exercise in humanity.

But, if it's nothing, nothing but a normal human experience, like eating, with endorphins and dopamine and chemicals released in the brain, why do sexual molestations and rapes have such a lasting emotional and spiritual impact on the students I serve?

Why are so many girls and guys regretful of their decision to "fool around" with him/her?

In contrast, how come every romantic movie makes the sex scene the pinnacle moment of the intimate relationship?

It can't be both.

I've made a lot of dumb decisions in my life. But, one of my best decisions I've ever made was to give my virginity to my wife only after we were married.

I guess I'm just overwhelmed by the sheer number of lives destroyed by an unhealthy and/or immature sexual encounter.

I wonder how many of those encounters are initiated merely as a means to beat boredom.

Whatever your choices for your relationships, I guess I just want to say.

You're valuable.

Life is precious.

Sex is intimate and spiritual.

So ... Don't Settle.

Create

Most statistics are made up.

Probably like 87.26% of them. (Math joke-Did u get it?)

But I've heard that 3% of the people create the culture that the other 97% passively experience.

I believe we can change the world.

But, it won't happen by simply being a passive observer of all that's happening.

It's time for you to join the 3%.

One of my favorite quotes is by Peter Diamandis — "The best way to predict the future is to create it."

And that's what I'm calling you to do.

You create the future, even the present.

You are a cultural architect re-creating the world by what you dream, believe is possible, and bring people together to make a reality.

When you collaborate, the vision will get better and sometimes worse depending on the voices in the project.

You will constantly be dreaming, collaborating, reimagining, exploring and improving, and creating again.

It's work. It's frustrating. It's messy.

But, it's also inspiring.

It's worth doing.

Create something better. Don't just be a spectator.

And don't wait. Show the world your best self.

Start today.

Failing

It's inevitable. You will fail and fail often on the path to doing something meaningful. It does not change your identity, unless you let it.

The other day my son had a meltdown.

Playing basketball in the driveway, he kept missing the baskets that were too high for him to hit continually.

His little arms were still developing. Fatigue was setting in and he couldn't push the ball all the way to the hoop.

Being a little conqueror that hates to lose, he started crying ... And throwing stuff ... And stomping his foot ... And screaming.

It was ugly!

After a few minutes he was calm again and I asked him why he was so upset.

Through tear-filled eyes he looked at me and said, "I'm a loser."

It hurt my heart. Literally.

He's wrong but he doesn't know it. And it doesn't matter if he's wrong or right if he believes it.

It made me angry that such a bold-faced lie would enter his head. He did not have enough experience knowledge or understanding to qualify him to make any determination of his ability to be a basketball player.

But, even if he were right, failure or weakness in one area should not define him in every area of his life.

Being a poor basketball player does not define anyone as a loser.

But it reminded me of the students and young adults I serve.

You have not experienced enough of the world to make a broad sweeping judgment about your capability, much less such a disparaging remark about your identity.

I kneeled down and looked my little son in the eyes and said, "Look at me."

"Son, that is a lie! You are not a loser. You are a conqueror. You're a winner. The fact that you are getting worse is only because you pushed yourself so hard to become better. Usually, when you want to become better at something, you get worse before you get better as you go through the learning curve. You may feel like a loser ... I understand. But, I know you. I see you. And you're not losing. You're learning."

The same goes for you. Stop defining yourself by your present shortcomings.

As you passionately go out to make your mark on the world, you WILL experience failure that will cause you to question your newfound identity and zeal.

Don't quit. Don't redefine yourself.

You're not losing. You're learning.

Push through it.

Everything I Said In 476 Words

In Part One of this book you learned to see boredom in a new light.

You looked at boredom from the angles of the feelings of that person sharing boredom's impact on their life on social media.

It's painful, emotional, frequent, and often lonely.

You've also seen it from the perspective from those who claimed to have its cure.

They claimed you should ignore it as part of growing up, find something to do, get a job, find more friends.

We learned that none of these cultural "cures" actually work. They all delay and fail to understand boredoms role in your life.

Finally, you've seen it from the perspective of those who ran from boredom indiscriminately into the arms of the destructive vices that surround us.

Through some of these tragic and senseless stories, you learned when you take ownership of an identity, true or false, you will tend to act consistently with who that identity tells you that you are.

You believe the reflection in the mirror.

You've watched with me how the cycle repeats itself day after day in the individual lives of culture in its repetitious and never-ending cycle.

Finally you learned what it is.

It is the single greatest indicator of the single most important problem in young adult culture today, a Visionless life.

But you also learned it can be beaten. Once you defeat boredom, you never have to deal with it's nuisance again.

In Part 2 of the book, you began to answer the question that boredom demands an answer to: Who are you?

You began to see yourself, not in light of the reflections you've already seen in the mirror, but in the reflections you've yet to experience.

Hopefully you came away from your exploration of you with an understanding of your identity as one of someone with meaningful values that inspire you and the world around you.

You learned some of the steps you can take, as you dream, explore, collaborate, and create to make your dreams of a better world and an awesome life a reality.

I cannot promise you fame and fortune by beating boredom. This is just the first step. But by making a decision, by taking a risk and stepping into the unknown, by planting your flag and declaring that you are going to do something bigger and scarier than even you thought possible, you've now become something you never were.

You're going to a new level, a new level to which you've never been.

Welcome to the great adventure.

Now you are on an epic journey and you are at the center of an epic fight for good.

Who will you bring along? What villains will you conquer?

How will you change the world?

It's up to you now. You can live an awesome life now.

I cannot wait to hear your story.

Conclusion

While you're given gifts and callings or maybe a sense of destiny some would say, the truth of the matter is, in all of this you choose.

You get to choose.

It sounds cliché, and maybe it is, but you cannot choose what will happen to you but you can choose how you will respond and who you will be in light of that.

I found that many people are ignorant of the fact that they get to choose.

But that is exactly what boredom forces you to do. To choose.

In that choosing, more often than not, I found that people settle.

They settle for the relationships that do not inspire them by picking out a couple of good points, they settle for an occupation that does not inspire them in the name of survival or urgency.

They make mistakes that set them back and as they look in the mirror and see the reflection of failure staring back at them, they believe what they see.

They settle for its identity in their life.

But, I want to ask you to dream.

I want to ask you to ignore the reflection staring back on you on the basis of your past and to look forward to a future of unlimited possibility of new dreams of bigger dreams.

A dream in which despite your inconsistencies, together we can do something special with our lives.

I told you that we are always in pursuit of our best self. It's when we are living in that pursuit that we are perfect and beautiful.

When boredom demands that you answer the question, "Who am I?"

Perhaps the answer is, I am the one in pursuit of my best self.

I am the one chasing my calling. I won't wait.

In that journey, I will fight for good. I will fight to win and in the fight I will find out who I am and who I am not.

As of today, there is one thing I know I'm not:

I'm not bored.

EPILOGUE:

Change The World

I hope you liked the book.

I hope you're inspired to change the world too!

I'd love for you to check out a movement that's working to-gether to make a difference all over the world.

Come check us out at www.CTWUniversity.com to receive some free goodies on how to find something you're passion-ate about and make a meaningful difference at the same time.

Also, follow me on social media:

Twitter/Periscope @JosephAaron.
Facebook.com/JosephAaronAuthor
Instagram – JosephAaron99

ABOUT THE AUTHOR

@JosephAaron is a Speaker, Author, and the Leader of a Student Movement that works with students and young adults to change the world in new and exciting ways.

Made in the USA
Columbia, SC
01 May 2018